W9-AXY-561

I CAN READ ABOUT

BATS

Written by Elizabeth Warren

Illustrated by Norman Nodel

Troll Associates

10 9 8 7 6 5 4 3 2

When you hear the word *bat,* do you think of ghosts and monsters? Some people do. That is because they do not really know about bats.

Don't be afraid.
There are many stories and tales about these
strange animals but, like many tales, most of
them are not true.

It is not true that
bats change shape during
the day and turn into bats
only at night.

It is not true that
you will have to shave your
head if a little brown bat
gets caught in your hair.

It is not true that bats bring bad luck. These are only superstitions. They are stories that someone made up.

Perhaps the strangest thing
about a bat is the way it looks.

It looks something like a furry
mouse with wings. But bats can fly
and mice cannot.

If you are thinking, "Well then, bats must be like birds," you are mistaken. For although bats can fly, they are very different from birds.

Their bodies are covered with fur instead of feathers.
Their wings are covered with thin skin.

All bats belong to a group of animals called mammals. Squirrels and rabbits, horses and cows, lions and tigers and people are mammals, too. But of all the mammals, bats are the only mammals that can fly.

Baby bats do not hatch from
eggs. They are born alive
like puppies and kittens.
While they are young, their
mothers feed them with milk.

A bat's world looks quite different from that of other animals. That is because it spends so much of its time hanging upside down.

The little brown bat and other bats who live in the
United States, Canada, and parts of Europe are insect
eaters. They eat flies, mosquitoes, beetles and moths.
They swoop down and catch the insects in mid-air.

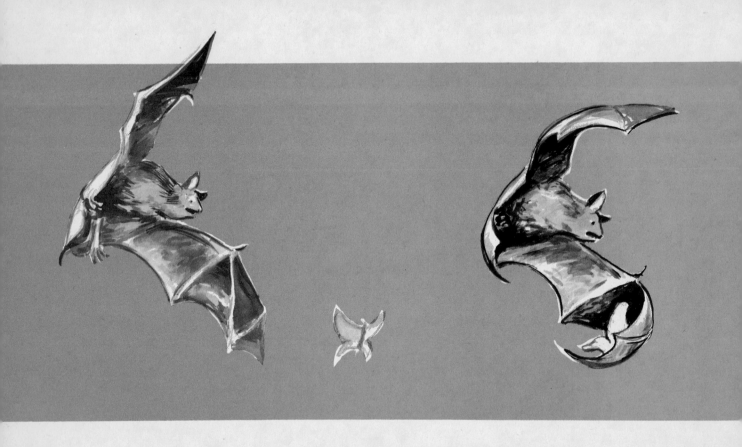

Some bats catch insects in their mouths. Other bats spot an insect,

swoop down, and catch or scoop the insect in the folds of their wings first.

In other parts of the world, there are
bats who eat fish. In the tropics
the hare-lipped bat flies over lakes and
rivers and catches small fish with
its sharp claws.

Flying foxes or fruit bats
prefer to eat fruit. In Central
and South America, banana growers
must pick their bananas while
still green, if they want
to stay ahead of the
bats.

There are even bats that sip nectar from
flowers. The long-nosed bat searches
for night-blooming plants and trees.
Then, it sticks its long, thin
tongue into the blossoms and
drinks the sweet nectar.

In parts of Asia, there lives a large and
terrible bat. The cannibal bat eats not
only insects and fruit but birds, mice,
rats and smaller bats as well.
It is no wonder that other
bats do not like to
roost, or stay
nearby.

Most frightening of all is the vampire bat.
The vampire bat lives in Central and South America.
It feeds only on the blood of mammals and birds.

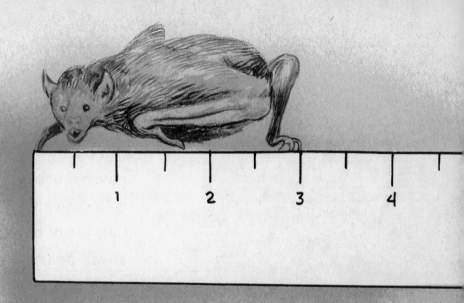

    Most vampire bats are only about three inches long.
They have very small, sharp teeth and long tongues.
Although they live on blood, vampire bats usually
make small wounds. Sometimes they do not even
wake sleeping animals.

The most amazing thing about bats is how they find their way in the dark. They can fly through a forest and never touch a branch. Entire colonies can whisk through the darkest of caves and never hit a wall or another bat. At high speed, they can catch tiny insects.

How do they do it?

They do not depend on their
eyes to find their way.

By tying blindfolds on bats, scientists
proved that it was not their eyesight that
guided them. In total darkness, the bats
were still able to find their way without
making a mistake.

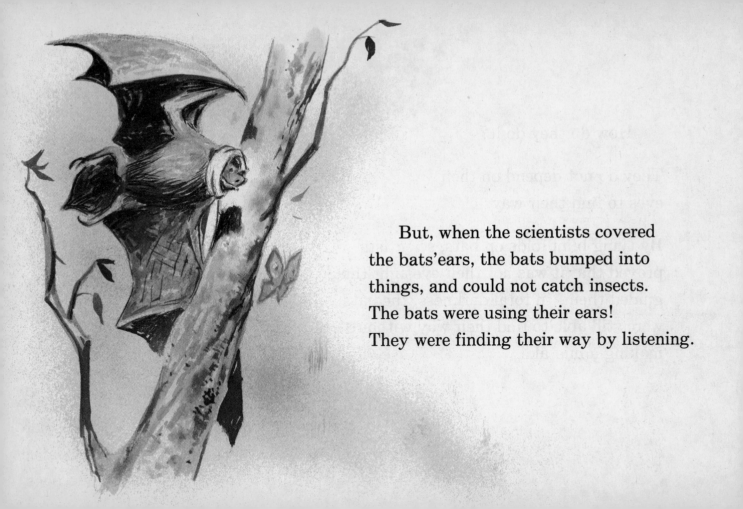

But, when the scientists covered
the bats' ears, the bats bumped into
things, and could not catch insects.
The bats were using their ears!
They were finding their way by listening.

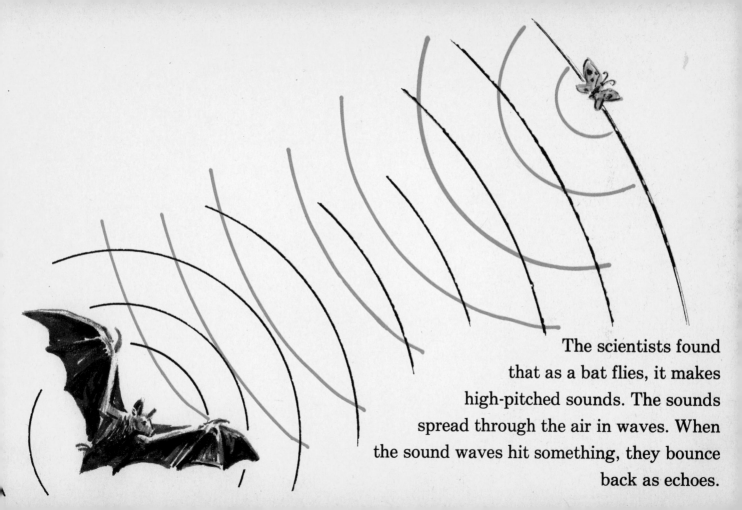

The scientists found
that as a bat flies, it makes
high-pitched sounds. The sounds
spread through the air in waves. When
the sound waves hit something, they bounce
back as echoes.

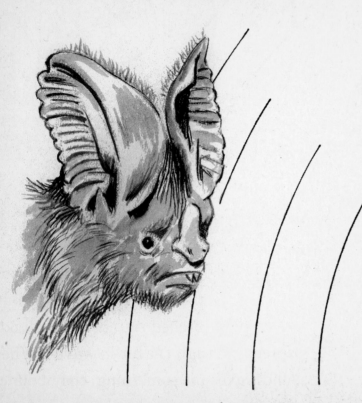

When the bat hears the echoes,
it knows how far away the moth is.
By listening to the echoes, it knows
how far away a tree is.

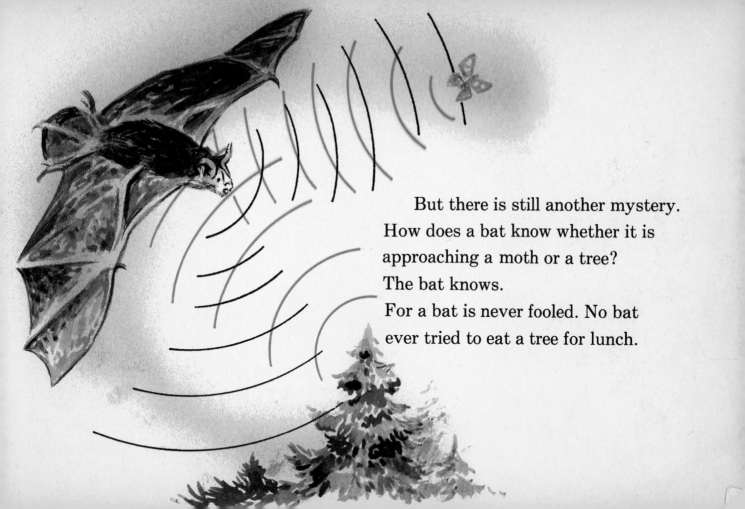

But there is still another mystery.
How does a bat know whether it is
approaching a moth or a tree?
The bat knows.
For a bat is never fooled. No bat
ever tried to eat a tree for lunch.

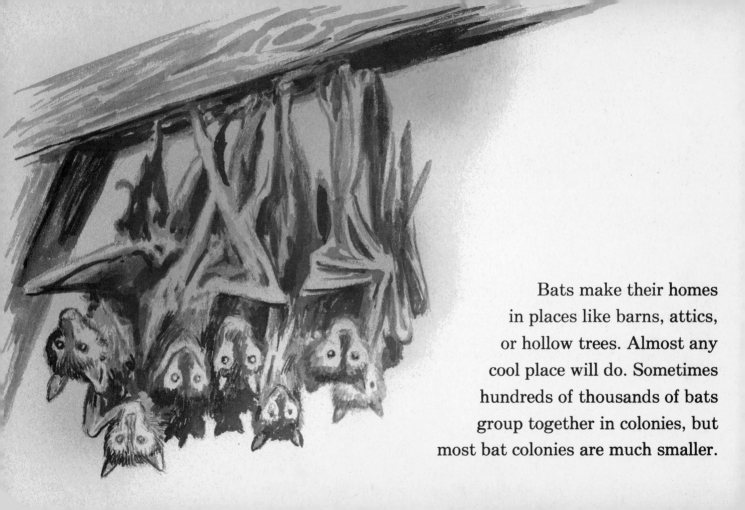

Bats make their homes in places like barns, attics, or hollow trees. Almost any cool place will do. Sometimes hundreds of thousands of bats group together in colonies, but most bat colonies are much smaller.

Bats about to give birth, and mothers with small babies often live together and form colonies of their own.

Baby bats are born in late spring. They are so tiny they weigh only a fraction of an ounce.

Hanging by their wings, mothers often rock babies in their tails.

Some babies go everywhere with their mothers. Soon after they are born, they cling to her fur with their teeth and tiny claws as she goes flying through the night air in search of food.

Other young bats are left hanging in the roost.
Thousands of them are left hanging like bunches of
grapes. But each mother, upon returning, is able
to find her own baby.

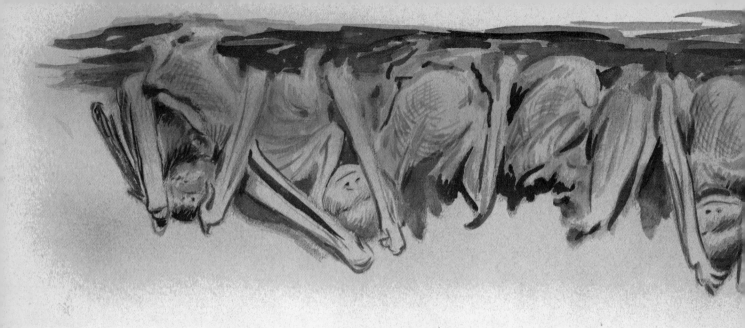

Bats eat twice as much food as they need. Half the food is stored away as body fat. It is used when food is scarce, or in the winter when the bat goes into a deep sleep called *hibernation*.

When a bat is hibernating, its breathing and heartbeat nearly stop. The fat that has been stored lasts for six to seven months, until it is time for the bat to wake up.

All bats do not hibernate.
Some fly to a warmer climate to spend the winter.
In the springtime, thousands of them
fill the sky as they return to their old roosts.

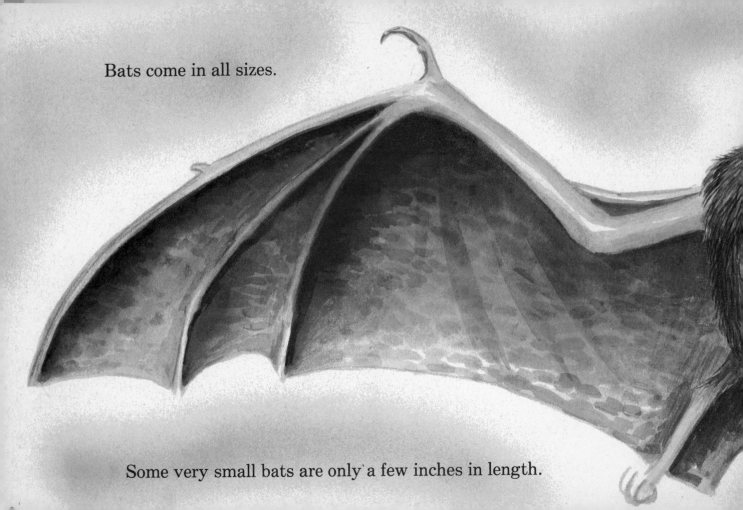

Bats come in all sizes.

Some very small bats are only a few inches in length.

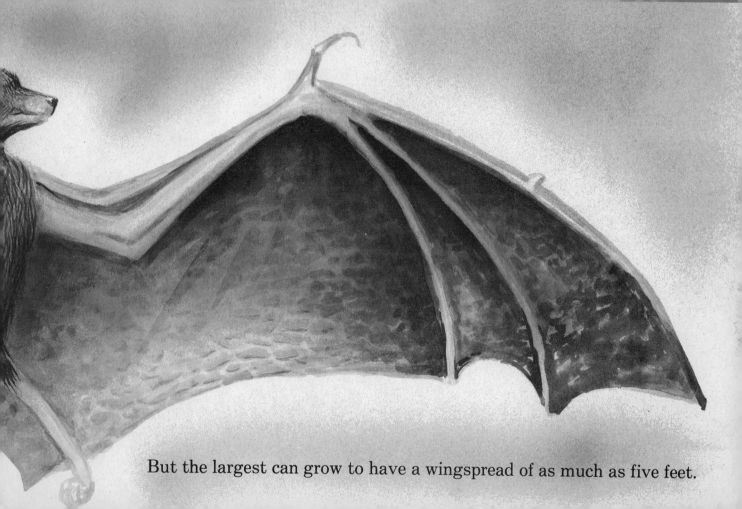

But the largest can grow to have a wingspread of as much as five feet.

There are millions and millions of bats in North America alone.

Although you should not pick up a bat, most bats are valuable friends to man. They eat insects that cause damage to crops and trees. In just a few hours, a hungry bat can eat its own weight in moths, flies, mosquitoes, and gnats.

Perhaps one summer night, after the sun goes down, you will see a little bat flying in the evening . . . its dark shape blurring in the warm summer sky.